WHAT DO ROOTS Do?

by
KATHLEEN V. KUDLINSKI

illustrated by
DAVID SCHUPPERT

NORTHWORD
Minnetonka, Minnesota

The illustrations were created using airbrush, oils, and acrylics
The text and display type were set in Shannon and Nyx
Composed in the United States of America
Designed by Lois A. Rainwater
Edited by Kristen McCurry

Text © 2005 by Kathleen V. Kudlinski
Illustrations © 2005 by David Schuppert
Hardcover edition ISBN-13: 978-1-55971-896-7
Paperback edition ISBN-13: 978-1-55971-980-3
First paperback printing: 2007

Books for Young Readers
11571 K-Tel Drive
Minnetonka, MN 55343
www.tnkidsbooks.com

The Library of Congress has cataloged the hardcover edition as follows:

Kudlinski, Kathleen V.
What do roots do? / by Kathleen V. Kudlinski ; illustrated by David Schuppert.

p. cm.

ISBN 1-55971-896-X (hardcover)
1. Roots (Botany)--Juvenile literature. I. Schuppert, David. II. Title.

QK644.K79 2005

581.4'98--dc22   2004031119

Printed in Singapore
10 9 8 7 6 5 4 3 2

For my wonderful kids,
Betsy and Henry,
grown strong and separate
on intertwined roots
—K. V. K.

To my wife, Patti,
and my children, Stephanie, Nathan,
Sarah and Rebecca,
for their inspiration and encouragement;
and to Harley,
my golden retriever who was always beside me
—D. S.

What do roots do for their plants up above?
They hold them up straight when the wind gives a shove.
They hold them upright when the ground's on a slant.
They hold them in place if you play on the plant.

How else do they use
this underground link?
Plants are all thirsty.
They use roots to drink.

The roots branch out small, then tinier still.
Then teeny root hairs drink the thirsty plant's fill.
Roots suck water in, then they send it up high,
through tubes far too tiny to see with your eye.

Water flows up through rootlets,
then taproots...

...and trunk,
then branches...

...and twigs,
until each leaf's drunk all the water it needs.
And then, way up there,
the rest blows away on a breeze, in the air.

Palm, pine, or maple,
it always is true—
half of the tree
will be hidden from you.

Shadowed by treetops,
green ferns and moss grow.
So do their roots
in the darkness, below.

In sunny yards full of grass, weeds, and clover,
you could see all the roots if you turned the dirt over.
But you wouldn't do that. It wouldn't be wise!
When you break off its roots, a plant often dies.

Your garden is brightest
and makes the most flowers
when the roots have been watered
by hose or by showers.

Food grows in the garden, in vegetable row.
Some ripens in sunshine, but some hides below.
Carrot and radish, potato and beet—
the underground root is the part that we eat!

The roots of a cactus
spread far to the sides
or reach deep in soil
for water that hides.

And even in ponds
water lilies have found
the best way to grow
is with roots in the ground.

So under each tree
is a tree made of roots,
and under each rose
and beneath bamboo shoots.
Whenever you look
at a plant short or tall,
remember, you don't see
the whole thing at all.

KATHLEEN V. KUDLINSKI's first love was nature. She taught science in elementary schools for seven years and she is now the author of thirty-two books and a prize-winning newspaper columnist. A Master Teaching Artist for the State of Connecticut, she visits classrooms as often as possible. Ms. Kudlinski lives beside a deep, wild lake in Guilford, Connecticut.

DAVID SCHUPPERT studied art at The Studio School of Art & Design and The School of Art & Design, both in Philadelphia. He's an award-winning artist with a wide range of mediums and themes— from natural science and wildlife to portraits and military art. His work has been featured in children's books, medical texts, advertisements, and even on vehicles! Mr. Schuppert lives with his family in Taylors, South Carolina.